This book is presented
in honor of

THE FRIENDS OF THE MORAGA LIBRARY

by

Moraga Branch, Contra Costa County Library

PORCUPINES

PORCUPINES

PETER MURRAY

THE CHILD'S WORLD

In the late fall, after the trees have lost their leaves, you take a walk through the woods. Squirrels jump from branch to branch, chattering loudly. A deer watches as you walk past. It stands so still you don't even know it is there. You are looking up at the trees, searching for something dark and prickly.

There it is, high on the trunk of a tree. It looks like a bird's nest. You wait, watching carefully. Soon, it starts to move down the tree trunk. You've found a porcupine!

The porcupine moves slowly. Porcupines are rarely in a hurry. There is plenty of time for everything, if you are a porcupine! It climbs down to the ground and waddles toward you. Porcupines have poor eyesight. It probably doesn't even know you are there. You watch it shuffle through the leaves, intent on porcupine business. Maybe it's going to take a nap in its den—an old, hollow log. Or maybe it's just looking for another tree to climb.

Like beavers, squirrels, and mice, porcupines are members of the *rodent* family. All rodents have four chisel-shaped teeth called *incisors*. The porcupine uses these long, sharp teeth to gnaw on tree bark. Porcupines are one of the largest North American rodents. They can weigh up to forty pounds and grow to over three feet long!

The porcupine looks like a big, fluffy teddy bear, but you don't want to pet it! Underneath its long, dark hairs the porcupine has a secret weapon.

Suddenly, the porcupine stops. It can't see very well, but it can smell you! The porcupine arches its back, and thousands of long, sharp, silvery quills stand straight up in the air. It shakes its body back and forth, and the quills make a rattling sound. It growls and chatters its teeth. The porcupine is saying, "Go away!" It turns its back to you and swishes its tail back and forth. The tail is loaded with sharp quills. This porcupine is mad!

The porcupine's quills are its main defense against predators. Porcupines cannot shoot their quills, but they can swat an attacker with their quill-covered tails. Each quill is two to three inches long and very, very sharp. The quill has tiny barbs that make it difficult to remove. If it is not pulled out right away, the quill works its way deeper and deeper into the predator's body. A face full of porcupine quills can eventually kill even large animals such as wolves and mountain lions.

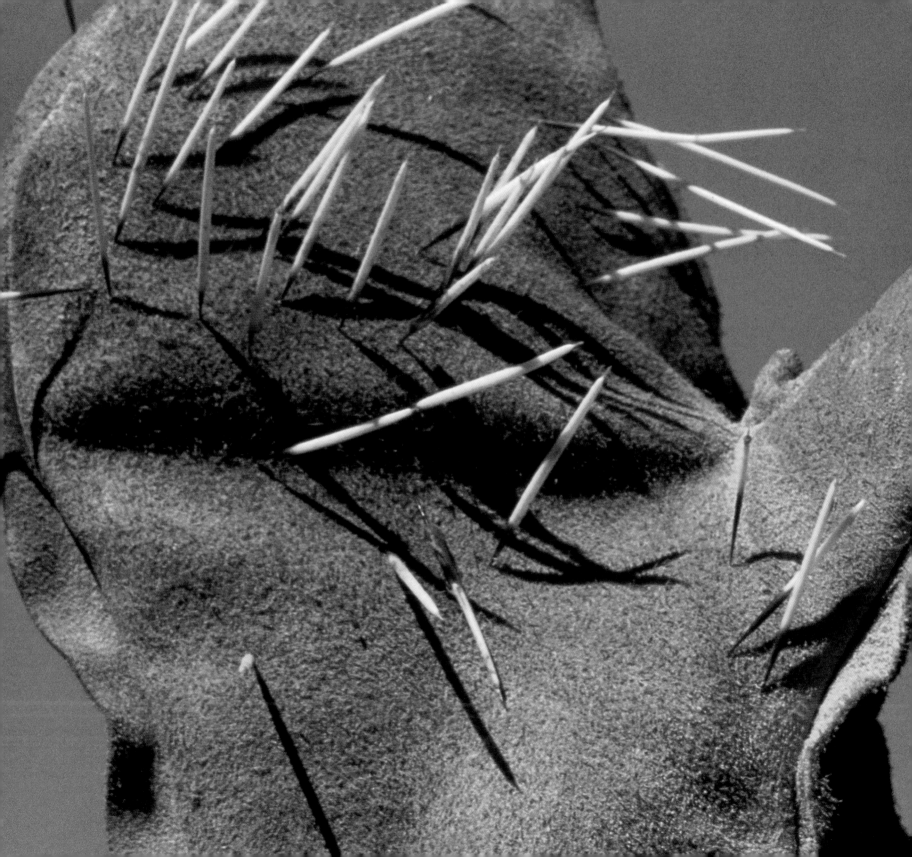

Most animals know enough to leave porcupines alone, but there is one animal that is not afraid of the porcupine's quills—the fisher. The fisher is a member of the weasel family. It looks like a cat with a pointy nose. Fishers are smaller than porcupines, but they are very fast and very strong. The attacking fisher jumps back and forth in front of the porcupine. The porcupine turns around and around, trying to strike with its prickly tail, but the fisher is too fast! Soon, the porcupine is so dizzy and tired it can't defend itself. The fisher finally attacks the porcupine's head, where there are only a few quills.

Exactly how many quills does a porcupine have? One scientist tried to find out, but there were too many quills to count! After a while he gave up and guessed that each porcupine has about 30,000 quills. Anyone who doesn't believe it is welcome to find their own porcupine and start counting!

Porcupine quills are hollow, so they don't weigh very much. These hollow, air-filled quills make porcupines excellent swimmers. When a porcupine sees a water lily, it jumps right in the water and swims out for a snack.

In the winter, porcupines eat tree bark. During the warmer months, they eat leaves, grasses, shoots, roots, and flowers. They also like fresh fruit and vegetables. Farmers sometimes trap or shoot porcupines to prevent damage to their crops.

Porcupines love salt. They'll chew on just about any-thing that tastes salty. Sometimes campers are surprised to wake up in the morning and find the handles of their canoe paddles chewed off! Salty perspiration soaks into the wooden handles, attracting hungry porcupines.

Porcupines might look clumsy when they waddle along on the ground, but they are expert tree climbers. Sharp claws and rough pads on their feet help them grip the bark. When a porcupine wants to get back to the ground, it climbs down backwards, using the stiff bristles on the bottom of its tail to help it balance. Porcupines are careful climbers, but even the best climbers make mistakes. Fortunately, when a porcupine falls, its quills cushion the landing and the animal is usually unhurt.

Porcupines are usually slow, quiet animals. In the late fall, however, they start to act a little crazy. They chatter and stomp their feet and chase one another. They make strange whining noises. The male porcupines wrestle with each other. When porcupines wrestle, they do it very carefully. Even porcupines don't like getting stuck with quills! This odd behavior is part of the porcupine mating ritual. Soon, each female chooses a mate. The male and female stay together for only a few days. After mating, the male leaves and the female returns to her den.

A few months later, the female porcupine gives birth to one baby. A baby porcupine is called a *porcupette*. The porcupette's quills are soft at birth, but they quickly harden. Within an hour, the porcupette is fully protected by thousands of hard, sharp quills.

A porcupette quickly learns to get about on its own. In two days, it is climbing high in the trees. Within two weeks, it is nibbling tender leaves and grasses. The porcupette stays with its mother for about two months.

The North American porcupine is one of more than thirty different porcupine species. One of the biggest and most dangerous porcupines lives in Africa. The African crested porcupine has quills fifteen inches long. When it turns its back to you and raises its quills, you'd better look out! This porcupine has been known to charge backwards!

Another unique porcupine is found in South America. The tree porcupine, which lives deep in the tropical rain-forest, has a *prehensile* tail—it can wrap its tail around a branch and hang from it like a monkey!

Porcupines are common across the northern United States and Canada, but because they are active mostly at night, they are seldom seen. Some people think porcupines are pests because they damage trees, orchards, and gardens. But in their forest habitat, porcupines are a healthy part of the natural environment.

Some people like porcupines so much they keep them as pets. A pet porcupine is friendly and playful, but you must be very, very careful when you pet it!

INDEX

birth, 26

claws, 23

climbing, 23

defenses, 12

dens, 6, 25

enemies, 12, 15

eyesight, 6

feet, 9, 23, 25

fishers, 15

food, 19

mating, 25

pets, 30

porcupettes, 26

rodents, 9

salt, 20

sense of smell, 10

size, 9

sleeping, 6

species, 29

swimming, 19

tails, 10, 15, 23, 29

teeth, 9-10

walking, 6, 23

PHOTO RESEARCH
Charles Rotter/Archipelago Productions

PHOTO CREDITS
COMSTOCK/George Lepp: 2
E. R. Degginger: 31
Frank Todd: 28
Jeanne Drake: front cover, 7, 8, 11, 21
Joe McDonald: 14
Leonard Lee Rue III: 13, 22, 27
Paul Rezendes: 18, 24
W. Perry Conway: 4, 17

Library of Congress Cataloging-in-Publication Data
Murray, Peter, 1952 Sept. 29-
Porcupines / Peter Murray.
p. cm.
Summary: Describes the physical characteristics,
behavior, and life cycle of porcupines.
ISBN 1-56766-019-3
1. Porcupines--Juvenile literature.   [1. Porcupines.]   I. Title.
QL737.R652M87   1993   93-22833
599.32'34--dc20

Distributed to schools and libraries in the United States by
ENCYCLOPAEDIA BRITANNICA EDUCATIONAL CORP.
310 South Michigan Avenue
Chicago, Illinois 60604